TRADITIONAL ESTATE PLANNING IS FINISHED

(A Refined Focus On Modern Asset Protection)

Attorney Jeffrey Hall, MBA, CPA, Esq.

Ordering Information:

Quantity sales. Special discounts are available on quantity purchases by corporations, associations, and others. For details, contact the author at the address below.

Orders by U.S. trade bookstores and wholesalers. Please contact the Law Office of Jeffrey Hall, Inc. at Tel: (925) 230-9002 or visit www.HallLawGroup.com.

Printed in the United States of America

Published in 2019

ISBN: 978-1-946481-81-8

FOREWORD

Today most estate plans are woefully outdated and dangerous in that they do not protect the assets of families. Why, because most estate plans were drafted with two primary objects in mind, one is to protect against probate and the other is to protect against estate taxes. Estates are presently taxed at $11 million per individual; although the federal law is expected to sunset that number down to 3.5 million in 2026, yet most clients either individually or married are not near that amount and taxes are therefore mainly irrelevant. The other issue is probate and although, it can be costly, the expenses incurred are nowhere near the devastation of long-term care expenses and other pre-mortem events, such as a beneficiary getting divorced with the exposure of litigation from an ex-spouse creditor, or perhaps dad dies and mom remarries a man who cleverly gets mom to sign a deed to property out of the trust and into Joint tenancy with right survivorship. The secondary concern that I raise in this forward is that the real risk to the loss of assets is not estate taxes and probate; the real threat is from the pre-mortem human activity that affects an estate plan. With life expectancy a century ago at 50 years of age for the average man yet today life expectancy has reached the low to mid-90s with the advent of modern technology such as by-pass surgery, pace-makers, and many other sophisticated medical devises and medications that keep people alive years well beyond their natural biological life span. So, the good news is that we're living longer but the problem is that most of us haven't prepared properly for this longer life and its affect upon our assets and our estate plans. Published statistics report that those aged 65 and older can anticipate a 50% probability of spending some time in a long-term care facility (LTC) at approximately $10,000 month per month. Statistics also report that if we live to our mid-80s, we can expect a 70% likelihood of matriculating into an LTC. Further, we've learned that most LTC convalescence services focus mostly with mental issues such as Alzheimer's and dementia diseases. These types of illnesses can often lead to very long periods of tenancy in LTC facilities. Many live well past 10 to 12 years in LTC with an average monthly cost of $10,000 to $15,000 (for memory care services) and that can last for over a decade. Some might recall President Ronald Reagan who lived with dementia for over 12 years before his death in 2004. So, you can see what the real risk is regarding protecting assets. The risk is primarily pre-mortem lack of planning and the post-mortem planning is easy to analyze but again, that's not where the risk is.

This forward was written to highlight the focus of this book on issues that are mainly the true threat to our financial health and its affect within our estate plan consultation and planning. I'll speak very little regarding issues of estate taxes and probate costs as they're immaterial to the real costs and risks of aging. And so now we go forward…

DEDICATION

To my beloved mother, Margaret, a second-generation Irish woman who lived much of her life in Queens, New York. She had a work ethic that would rival most, she worked like an immigrant and never complained. I observed her during my early years and learned quickly that life was not for the slackers. She was dedicated to her work as an accountant/bookkeeper, whatever it might be, she gave it all she had.

To my family, whom I work tirelessly every day, but most importantly to my amazing beloved wife, Laura Rose, who consistently inspires me with her love, relentless support, and wonderful spirit and friendship.

To my beautiful daughter Courtney Rose, who provides a hug, a big kiss, and "dad—you can do it." I'm blessed.

ACKNOWLEDGEMENTS

I acknowledge all my clients who have shared much of their lives with me, both the sublime and the dark. I desire to provide information to those who are thinking of designing an estate plan and more importantly to those who are seeking the advice of an attorney to assist with the design of that estate plan. I take this obligation seriously and promise my clients that they'll get the most dedicated and focused lawyer who will design an estate plan that is best for their family.

DISCLAIMER

This publication is intended to be used for educational purposes only. No legal advice is being given, and no attorney-client relationship is intended to be created by reading this material. The author assumes no liability for any errors or omissions or for how this book or its contents are used or interpreted or for any consequences resulting directly or indirectly from the use of this book. For legal or any other advice, please consult an experienced attorney or the appropriate expert who is aware of the specific facts of your case and is knowledgeable of the law in your jurisdiction.

Law Office of Jeffrey Hall, PC
3478 Buskirk Avenue
Suite 1000
Pleasant Hill, CA 94523
www.halllawgroup.com
(925) 230-9002

TESTIMONIALS

"Jeff prepared my estate plan this past summer. Using thoughtful questions, he guided me through the process. I chose to work with him after reading many great reviews on several sites. I found him personable, reasonably priced, thorough, professional, and in a great nearby location in the event any future questions arise. At the end of the process, I left with a well-organized estate plan binder and felt good about having all my affairs in order."

— *Lydia F.*

****

"Mr. Hall was friendly, accommodating, professional and easy to work with in producing our living trust. He was responsive and available in answering all of our questions. He was patient in explaining the legalese. He followed through from start to finish in a timely manner. He was thorough and very organized. We highly recommend him, as we "trust" him."

— *Steve and Carol I.*

****

"Jeff helped me with my capital gains within a trust issue. His knowledge base is excellent, saving me hours of unfruitful phone calls and frustration. Jeff offered several suggestions to optimize a desired outcome. His rates are very reasonable. As trust litigation is very complex, you need somebody that knows the law and is able to resolve an issue without the expensive and extraneous letters back and forth that only rack up billable hours. You can count on Jeff to be your advocate."

— Phil P.

****

"My wife received an inheritance and we needed to update our estate. We worked with Mr. Hall previously and he did a spot on great job. Mr. Hall covered all issues of my wife's inheritance, such as title changes and filing affidavits with the records office. He was awesome and we are glad to one again recommend Mr. Hall."

— Brian D.

****

"Jeff is hands down one of the most personable and knowledgeable lawyers I've ever worked with. Right from the start, it's obvious that Jeff truly cares about his clients and their wellbeing. He is my #1 recommendation for estate planning????"

— Colin P.

****

"Very knowledgeable! I called with a probate/will question and he was able to guide me in the right direction over the phone. I will certainly go to Jeff for my own estate planning. Thank you very much!"

— Richard R.

****

Table of Contents

ABOUT THE AUTHOR

Attorney Jeffrey Hall, MBA, CPA, Esq. is an experienced elder law & estate planning attorney whose practice is located in northern California, more specifically, the East Bay of San Francisco.

Jeffrey Hall provides sound legal advice and counsel for older adults and their families. Jeff believes that the maze of aging care and cost challenges can be addressed by proper planning and meeting issues straight on; he believes that planning and advocating for families may help provide more lifestyle choices and care options. Mr. Hall's own story includes the personal journey he faced when planning for care and financial concerns for his own mother following her health crisis. After working to resolve the many issues involving his mother's care, he decided to pursue advocacy for the elderly should be his priority and he then embarked on combining an elder law team that focuses on holistic planning involving legal, financial, and care concerns.

Mr. Hall didn't follow the traditional path to practice law. Indeed, Mr. Hall grew up in central Los Angeles during the 1960's and 70s with no expectation he would attend college, and law school was simply not an option. However, after completing his bachelor's degree in Economics from Saint Mary's College, he volunteered with the Air Force in 1981 and served for 9 years, both reserve and active. Upon returning to California, he and his wife made Pleasant Hill, California their home and have remained since. Thereafter, he worked 15 years, holding senior management positions in public and corporate accounting. While working full-time, he attended night school to earn his graduate degree in accounting and then passed the CPA exam.

In 1991, he transferred from the Air Force Reserve to the U.S. Coast Guard Reserve and served with distinction on board the High Endurance Cutter, USCGC Sherman (Alameda, CA), for three years and subsequently with the Joint Force—Naval Coastal Warfare Unit One-Eleven (Alameda, CA) with four tours to South Korea. Thereafter, Mr. Hall was assigned to the USCG Judge Advocate General (JAG) unit in Alameda, CA (from 2011 through 2014 and later in Seattle, WA (from 2014 through 2016) where he held the Senior Reserve Officer position (Reserve Commanding Officer) for all USCG JAG attorneys in the U.S. from 2011 through 2014. Mr. Hall retired from the USCG as a Commander after serving 25 years.

During his civilian work, he later attended law school (again, while working full-time) and became a licensed attorney in 2003. With his extensive experience in both business and taxation, he had a natural interest in estate planning and business law.

Today, Mr. Hall is a very experienced and seasoned estate-planning attorney specializing in trusts, elder law, Medi-Cal planning, trust litigation, and estate administration. Attorney Hall frequently appears in Superior Court on matters concerning trust litigation, trust reformations, conservatorships, and probates. He is a frequent speaker and author of many published articles about estate planning and elder law. In 2019, Mr. Hall was selected as a "Super Lawyer" by Thomson Reuters. This is a highly prestigious recognition for any lawyer to receive and it represents the best of the Top 5% of estate planning attorneys in northern California.

Attorney Hall began his legal practice in 2003 and later joined a large mid-sized law firm in 2006 in the east bay where he managed that firm's estate planning practice through 2017. He maintains his affiliation with that firm but mostly serves clients in private practice. Mr. Hall holds a bachelor's degree in Economics from the Saint Mary's College of California, an MBA in Accounting and Taxation from Golden Gate University in San Francisco, and a JD from JFKU College of Law. He's been selected as one of California's Top 100 Estate Planning Attorneys in California by the American Society of Legal Advocates. He's received the "Hero Award" from the AIDS Legal Referral Panel of San Francisco for 10 years of dedicated pro bono service to people of special needs. He's also a member of The State Bar of California, U.S. District Court Eastern District, U.S. District Court Northern District,

U.S. Court of Appeals 9th Circuit, U.S. Court of Appeals for the Armed Forces, U.S. Court of Appeals for Veterans Claims, and the U.S. Supreme Court Bar.

Attorney Hall offers all prospective clients a free 30-minute telephone consultation. Call now at 925-230-9002 or visit www.HallLawGroup.com or schedule an appointment at info@HallLawGroup.com.

The Law Office of Jeffrey Hall, PC is a veteran-friendly and veteran-owned law firm.

CHAPTER 1

DO IT YOURSELF ESTATE PLANNING – PAY NOW OR PAY LATER

How many of you have pulled your own teeth or performed your own root-canal?

I hope that no one has ever been so foolish to do such a thing. However, when it comes to legal services; many in the general public seem to have a different perceptive. They have little fear of the consequences of their actions. Perhaps it's because drafting legal documents incorrectly doesn't result in immediate harm such as death, or that there's no immediate physical pain. Many say, "well let's give it the old college try, what could possibly go wrong?"

This chapter is intended to shed some light on the substantial mistakes Do-It-Yourselfers ("DIY") make and the legal consequences of doing so.

Understand that many commercials convey the impression that legal services are "merely" secretarial tasks which require very little knowledge or skill in the preparation of an estate plan. That anyone can do it, we in the legal profession have found an enormity of mistakes and resulting litigation directly as a result of these DIY document preparation firms that cause a substantial harm and a resulting disservice to the public.

These examples highlight the immense naiveté of someone who thinks that drafting their own legal documents is a smart and cost-effective thing to do. Some say, well, I'm good at what I do at my job and I suspect that therefore, I possess the talent similar to an experienced and accomplished lawyer/CPA. As an estate planning attorney, I've seen and experienced several DIY disaster stories that need to be shared with the public and that's why I wrote this chapter specifically on this topic. Mainly, to help the public from shooting themselves in the foot.

The consequences of making a mistake often will result in substantial tax and legal consequences that will last a lifetime to the beneficiaries.

Over the past ten years or so, we've seen an increase in the DIY mentally of the do-it-yourselfers and proliferation of DIY providers have surfaced in many professional fields ranging from tax preparation, real estate, and estate planning. These providers purport to provide, at low cost, the ability to prepare computer-drafted documents that may resemble professionally prepared documents. While these DIY providers offer tools to enable the DIY project, as with the home improvement industry, they should be used with extreme vigilance.

Those who want to replace proper professional advice with a do-it-yourself online document-preparation vendor in complex fields like estate planning, elder law and Medi-Cal planning should understand the consequences of their actions. One should understand that even those with reasonably sophisticated abilities should think again before venturing into complex subject matter to which they know very little and beyond their area of expertise. Consider David Kautter, Commissioner of the Internal Revenue Service who was quoted as saying that "after 30 years of tax practice, I would no more have the stupidity to prepare my own tax return than I would engage in flying a Boeing 747 from LAX to New York."

Hence, due to the growing number of DIY-Vendors and Tools - the number of DIY legal providers continues to proliferate.

DIY providers market their services as charging unusually low fees for documents that ordinarily would cost much more if produced by a skilled attorney. For example, there's a DIY-Vendor who charges $89 to draft a Last Will and Testament. Many in the legal profession have questioned whether these services are in effect the unauthorized practice of law. Several large DIY-Vendors have been sued in at least three states (Missouri, North Carolina and Connecticut) for violating those states' unauthorized practice of law statutes.

Many in the legal profession have commented that the danger of preparing one's estate plan utilizing any one of these DIY-Vendors is that they may fool clients into a false sense of security.

Is working with a DIY-Vendor right for you? In very limited instances it might be appropriate to do so. For example, if a person of modest assets in his name alone, and simply wants to leave his assets to his closest surviving relative, it may be appropriate and sensible to use an online service. However, individuals with even slightly complex circumstances, creating a Will online and making a mistake can have very substantial and long-lasting consequences.

For example, a Wisconsin resident chose to purchase low-priced Will form kit. He carefully handwrote his intended gifts into the document preparation software. Since the software didn't come with an attorney consultation nor a professional review of his completed papers, he didn't have it properly witnessed. Believing that his Will was legally effective, he then committed suicide thinking that he had properly prepared his Last Will and Testament. His heirs, however, paid the price for his mistake. In the lawsuit by the decedent's heirs against the DIY Will vendor, the trial court struggled to find a way to confirm his handwritten comments to the form. Under Wisconsin probate law, the language on the pre-printed form was not admissible because the Will was not properly signed by the Testator (most states require a Will to be signed in the presence of two witnesses). The Court's attempt to remedy the decedent's efforts, cost the family tens of thousands of dollars. At least the decedent never saw that enormous expenditure paid by his heirs as he passed away believing he had saved money.

Will a DIY Estate Plan Work After You're Gone? Every state has its promulgated list of requirements (or elements) that must be present for a Will or other estate planning document to be legally effective. A person who prepares his own Last Will must remember that the ultimate test of his/her efforts will <u>only occur after death</u>. At that point, the decedent's intentions are forever silenced and unchangeable. If he does prepare his Will on his own, it's likely no one will be able to explain his intentions.

Should I Hire an Experienced Estate Planning Lawyer? The Role of the Attorney is that of a counselor and advisor. The estate planning lawyer provides his/her technical expertise in drafting complicated documents. Most attorneys have extensive experience in counseling clients in complex matters. For example, most have helped couples sift through the various possible options in selecting a guardian for their children. That decision may appear rudimentary, but the "best" guardian candidate may not have the "best" spouse, or one who lacks financial experience. Spouses may disagree as to the choice of guardian. They may need advice to understand a guardian's role. The Counselor-at-Law plays an important role in these and many other estate planning discussions.

The failure to properly state dispositions. A proper Will must clearly state the testamentary intent to dispose of assets. The terms and provisions used must be dispositive in nature (a letter of instruction will not suffice). Those who draft their own Wills run the risk of using words, terms or wording that could lead the disposition to become ineffective. The failure to use words of "testamentary intention" could void the Will. But a non-lawyer wouldn't know that.

Tax issue and concerns. State and federal taxes imposed on estates change often and have become increasingly complicated. Congress recently increased the federal estate tax exemption to $11.4 million, but that lasts only through the end of 2026 after which the exemption amount sunsets to $3.5 million. Meanwhile California is reviewing the possibility of implementing a California estate tax of $3.5 million perhaps as early as 2020. Thoughtful planning needs to be done to achieve the tax savings through a detailed understanding of numerous options available to reduce estate taxes.

Special needs considerations. If a child suffers from a learning disability, or is vulnerable to the influence of people seeking to grab his inheritance? What will happen to his/her assets if a child is disabled and requires governmental assistance such as Medi-Cal? For parents with special needs children, specialized trust planning may be required to avoid risking a special needs child's public benefit. In fact, one estate planning attorney noted that when he informed a DIY-Vendor representative that he had a disabled child, the representative advised him that he needed a supplemental needs trust which Large DIY-

Vendor did not provide and that he would need to contact an attorney to prepare one for him. It is doubtful that a non-attorney would be aware of the need for such specialized planning and the consequences of its omission.

Choosing Between Hiring a DIY-Vendor or a Skilled Lawyer for Professional Consultation. Notwithstanding the previous issues and concerns, the cost of preparing a Last Will or Trust for many people may be prohibitive. Before any consumer comes to that conclusion, however, they should examine the potential fees of engaging proper counsel to assist in estate planning and the benefits (for example, peace of mind) that come with such assistance. Moreover, the consumer should consider his own ability to reduce the cost of estate planning by being prepared when meeting with his/her attorney during the initial meeting. This would include providing a comprehensive list of all assets and liabilities, a detailed list of all beneficiaries, the collection of relevant documents (deeds, beneficiary designations, prior Wills, etc.). Taking the time to prepare before the initial consultation can reduce costs.

My main concern for the public is that many will have a false sense of security in these documents not realizing the administrative doom, and the potential litigation and all the consequences which loom brightly on the horizon for the families and heirs of those who foolishly believe that buying a $76 Trust will protect their families upon their death. Bottom line, the average consumer should proceed with extreme caution when using DIY estate planning vendors as a substitute for a properly and professionally prepared plan.

CHAPTER 2

WHY I CHOSE ESTATE PLANNING AND ELDER LAW

I've been a licensed CPA for 25 years. I began my career with Peat Marwick Mitchell, which was one of the big eight CPA firms in San Francisco at that time. It was my first real job when I returned from the Air Force. I started in their audit department and then later transferred to Arthur Andersen in Oakland. I worked in their tax department for a number of years. While working there, I went to school at night to earn my Master's degree in accounting and tax law.

Then came law school and I found that a background in what I had accomplished in tax and accounting would be a good combination for estate planning. I did estate taxes and then the elder law side of my practice came about very quickly, as I passed the bar exam. My mother died within three months of me passing the bar exam. She was a smoker and was dying of lung cancer, but we didn't know that yet. I was able to share with her, before she died, that her son had passed the bar. I always felt grateful that my mother knew I became a lawyer before she died. I know it gave her some sense of pride that her son had done well.

My mother had two sons and her expectations for the two of us were very high. We grew up in Central Los Angeles in the 60s and 70s. There were gangs, drugs, and it was tough living. Taking the bus home from football practice at night was often a life and death situation. I grew up knowing how to watch the streets, watch my back, and take care of myself. I saw a lot of poverty and disparity in wealth among people in the various regions of Los Angeles. Life was often very difficult for most of us. Wealth was everywhere in Hollywood, but it was highly concentrated to very few people. Most of Los Angeles is poverty stricken.

My mom instilled a sense of pride in my brother and me and believed that we could get ourselves out of the inner city. It started with her insistence that we were going to go to college. There was no other option and that was the end of it. When I did make it through school and became a lawyer, I decided that I wanted to help people who are less fortunate than I am. I decided that I would truly help the disadvantaged and poor, and I've done that now for over 15 years as an estate planning and elder law attorney, serving military veterans. I am a veteran and retired as U.S. Coast Guard JAG officer in 2016.

I was in the military for a long time and I have true love and respect for the men and women who serve our country. I also provide pro bono work to the AIDS Legal Referral Panel in San Francisco. That organization champions the cause of many people suffering from HIV in the Bay Area and need legal assistance with conservatorships, probates, wills, and estate planning. I've done this for a number of years and have received the AIDS Legal Referral Panel "Hero Award" for outstanding service for over 10 years. It feels good. I try to help people because I came from a modest area and I know the struggle. There's a perception of affluence in the Bay Area, similar to Los Angeles, but there's a great deal of poverty.

Before my mother died, I tried to get her into a long-term care facility in San Francisco. I didn't really know anything about elder law at the time and I had just passed the bar. I wasn't even licensed yet. We were told that there were no Medi-Cal beds available, so my mom had to stay home. My wife and I did the best we could to take care of her and she died at home. As an elder law attorney, I've come to discover that those nursing homes lied to us about bed-availability. I thought that they would not accept Medi-Cal patients. I then became very motivated to become knowledgeable in the field of elder law. I didn't want that to ever happen to another family.

Elder law can split into different directions. One is litigation for long term care misbehavior and abuse. I didn't pursue litigation in my mom's case because I didn't know anything about it. Now, 16 years later, I know a lot about it, although my practice is not heavy in litigation. I'm primarily a transactional lawyer. As an accountant and CPA, that is where my skillset lies. I do practice trust litigation, although I seek out mediation as a better alternative.

My efforts have been focused mostly on helping the elderly with health issues who are on Medi-Cal or Medicaid, assisting with Medi-Cal eligibility, long term care, and working with veterans who receive VA benefits to find housing for their final days. I believe society owes our seniors, at a minimum, a comfortable place to lay their head and receive competent medical services before they die.

CHAPTER 3

PRE-MORTEM ESTATE PLANNING

You may have heard of a family wealth trust. People assume that only the rich need a family wealth trust in their estate plans. Those with large estates can certainly benefit from the inclusion of the family wealth trust in their estate plan, but so can those with moderate means. A family wealth trust is simply one of many estate planning tools and it can be used to protect assets from taxes and probate, while providing for future generations in the long run. Including at least one trust in your estate plan is something that many people choose to do because of the variety of benefits a trust can offer, such as allowing you to shelter assets from creditors.

A trust can also provide tax advantages and probate ordinances. A trust allows you to exert a certain amount of control over assets placed in the trust, long after you are gone, by creating trust terms that control how assets can be invested and used to gain the most tax benefits. You'll most likely need to create an irrevocable living trust. The advantage of that type of trust is that once the assets are transferred, they can't be touched by creditors. The downside, however, it is that you can't modify an irrevocable trust, once it takes effect.

The primary benefit of a family wealth trust is the ability to control assets long after your death. Using trust terms, you're able to guide future generations by deciding which trust assets can be used ahead of time. Another significant benefit is that the assets held by the trust will, assuming the trustee manages the assets, continue to grow after being transferred into the trust. This, in turn, grows your family wealth and insurance so that successive generations will benefit from your gifts.

CHAPTER 4

PROTECT YOUR ASSETS WHILE YOU ARE STILL ALIVE

Planning for postmortem is easy. What you have leftover is what you distribute to your heirs. However, to get to that postmortem period, one most protect their assets so they have something to gift. Often, the most important process of postmodern planning is really pre-mortem planning. As we age, the likelihood that we'll need some form of long term care rises. The average monthly cost of such care in northern California is about $10,000-$15,000 per month. If we're concerned about the surviving spouse not being impoverished to pay for the institutional spouse's costs, we plan while still alive, so that we can spare that surviving spouse the emotional stress of paying for the institutional loved one while also continuing to pay to maintain the household.

In order to keep the process of debt distribution orderly, we need to focus on pre-mortem planning, so that we have something to leave our heirs upon our deaths. Most importantly, we don't want to saddle our surviving spouse or our general estate with substantial unpaid medical bills. The number one reason, in my experience, for bankruptcy in the state of California is medical expense of long term care. Up to 90% of the unpaid medical expenses in this area are directed to the payment of long term care facilities. Even a high-wage earning family can't afford to make the payments, which average from $10,000-$15,000 per month.

Most of us want to leave that responsibility to either our surviving spouse or to our kids. Many families across this country are truly wiped out, financially, from having to private pay for Mom or Dad's long term care costs. The bills are not paid because the family doesn't have the money and then the deceased's estate files for bankruptcy. This is the most common scenario leading to a bankruptcy. If you're interested in postmortem distribution, you have to have something left to make a distribution. In order to have something remaining in the estate, most of the estate planning should be focused on pre-mortem because that's where you save your assets.

CHAPTER 5

WHY DO WE NEED AN ESTATE PLAN?

Everyone should have their own estate plan, if they want to direct where their assets will go upon their death. We all have family members; some we love and others we despise. If you do not take steps to plan for your estate, California steps in under Probate Code 6401 and takes care of it for you. The state will decide who gets your property, money, and belongings. I always suggest that clients set up a plan, even if they don't have families. We can set up a charitable remainder trust, so that the client can live comfortably on their interest and dividends. Upon that person's death, a charity that he or she chooses a can receive a nice cash gift upon the Settlor's death.

I once had a client who came into my office asking me whether I was experienced in trust administration, which is carrying out the provisions of a person's trust when that person dies. He confidently handed me a trust that his mother had prepared by an online DIY-Vendor trust company, which devised the entire interest of a very expensive home in a very pricey, very exclusive area. He was to inherit this property as his sole and separate property. The appreciated value was about $2 million. I reviewed the trust and realized that the trust was not signed by the Settlor, his mother. I quickly checked title to the house to see if it had been recorded into the trust and found that the property wasn't even funded. This person, who thought his mom had an effective trust prepared, had to be told that the trust was completely ineffective and she didn't execute a will.

When the trust was determined to be ineffective and she didn't produce a will, under the mistaken belief that the trust was effective, she died intestate. This client had three other siblings. The mother wanted to gift the expensive house to the youngest son. Unfortunately, through the probate process, a son who would have received a $2 million house as his sole and separate property now had to share that property with three other siblings. There are now four owners, all tenants in common, so instead of $2 million he inherited a $500,000 component of the house. That is why it is important to make sure that you have your estate plan reviewed by a professional attorney. Had she used an actual estate planning attorney, she would have known that she had to fund the trust. This could have been easily completed by notarizing the signature and recording the grant deed with the recorder's office.

It is common for non-lawyers who draft legal documents that have significant legal consequences. I'm dismayed with the state bar of California, which allows this incompetence that harms the public and does no service. My suggestion to the public is to spend a bit more and save your family a major headache. If you do it right, your kids will thank you forever. You get what you paid for. Engaging a trust litigation lawyer to petition the court to correct mistakes could run anywhere from $10,000-$15,000. A simple $2,000 -$2,500 estate plan can save thousands of dollars for your kids.

Most people don't understand that with a lawyer, you're not just buying paperwork. You're buying years of experience, training, and knowledge. It's truly remarkable that a person will spend a lifetime of hard work and then, when it comes to preparing a legally competent estate plan, choose the cheapest document preparation company around. I'm a champion against both DIY-Vendors and bargain-basement estate planning lawyers. There's a local lawyer in town who markets a full estate plan for $680 and that is just reckless. When you see a lawyer in your local community selling an estate plan at that price, you'll quickly know you're dealing with someone fresh out of law school with little or no experience. Stay away from new attorneys who should have started their career with a larger firm before going out on their own. You owe it to your family to get the best lawyer to prepare your plan. <u>You're not buying a widget, you're buying experience and you're going to pay a fair price for that</u>.

CHAPTER 6

REGULAR AND PRE-MORTEM ESTATE PLANNING

There really isn't a difference between estate planning and pre-mortem estate planning. Traditional estate plans draft documents that are executable upon the death of the settlor or the testator. Not long ago, many estate planning attorneys were producing documents to avoid estate taxes and probate. Avoiding probate is certainly a relevant objective but it's not that big of a deal when a person dies with minimal assets. Those you choose will receive their distribution as you've indicated usually within 18 months. As for the estate tax issue, there's effectively no estate tax for 99.99% of taxpayers. The estate tax exemption amount for married couples is a combined estate tax exemption of $22,800,000, as of 2019. A single individual will have an exemption of $11,400,000, as of 2019. It's simply not a concern for the vast majority of people anymore. Although these amounts will sunset in 2026 to $3.5 million, but nevertheless, this sunset amount is very generous.

The focus now is on asset protection because that's where you'll find the assets for purposes of postmortem distribution. There are three main areas of concern. One, long-term care planning. Two, blended family arrangements and three, asset protection for heirs who have potential credit issues, including divorce. Traditional estate plans distributed postmortem and worried about estate taxes and avoiding probate. Today, the real focus is on legacy preservation and pre-mortem planning, trust protectors, distribution trustees, and limited power of appointments.

Second marriages and blended families can make estate planning complicated. If you just title everything in joint tenancy with right of survivorship, the surviving spouse's kids may get everything while the other spouse's children get nothing. The industry is really getting away from traditional planning and focusing more on pre-mortem asset protection, so that if Mom or Dad survive and wind up in a new marriage, we can protect the assets for their legacy. We can streamline the trust by bringing in trust protectors, limited powers of appointment, and court trustees to make sure that the surviving new spouse is not up to any misbehavior.

CHAPTER 7

FAMILY WEALTH TRUST AND ITS USE

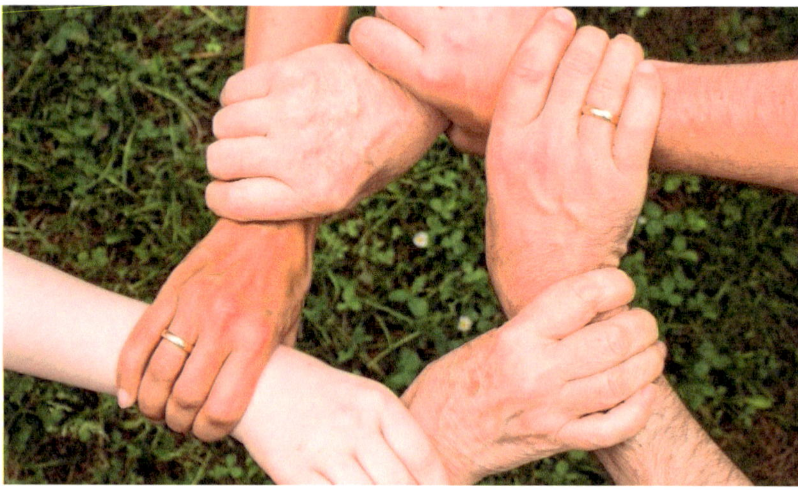

A family wealth trust can provide for and protect your heirs, along with passing on what I call values and wisdom. I always put a statement at the top of the trust as to why Mom and Dad are preparing their trust and why they've chosen this model of distribution. In the case of minors, a trust allows a parent to provide for a child without giving the child control over property. The parent can also mandate how and when the property can be distributed, and for what purposes. A family wealth trust can be a useful tool for taking care of heirs who have mental impairments or a lack of investment experience. The trust document can establish that all the money is controlled by a trustee with sound investment experience and judgment.

A trust preserves integrity of funds when the recipient has a history of extravagance. It can protect property from the heir's spendthrift nature, as well as from his or her creditors. This is also true for persons who feel pressured from their friends, financial advisors, and others who want a slice of the pie when someone comes into wealth. A family wealth trust can make it extremely difficult for a recipient to direct property to any one of these people. A spendthrift provision is the hallmark of a family wealth trust and is often used to further preserve the integrity of assets. It prohibits the heir from transferring his or her interests in a future distribution and also bars creditors from reaching into the trust.

Family wealth trusts are relatively easy to update, modify, and even revoke in some cases. A Last Will and Testament, however, is difficult to change and establishing one requires many formalities. Another benefit is the short circuiting of the order of probate. One popular benefit of the California family wealth trust is the avoidance of probate.

Property in the trust is not considered part of the estate, so it doesn't have to undergo this sometimes lengthy process. The property is instead administered and distributed by the trustee, according to the specific terms of the trust.

Probate expenses can be significant and vary according to the size of the estate and what it includes. It also varies by state and some have some very expensive and onerous procedures, while others are more streamlined versions of probate. Avoiding probate means not only avoiding hassles and expense, but also saving time. Probate can extend the amount of time before an heir can receive their inheritance by many years. Not only can it create hardship among the heirs but the property in the estate may also suffer.

Title companies and banks tend not to look favorably upon estates that have houses or commercial properties that are vacant while heirs litigate matters. You tend to end up with squatters and other issues. Assets must be carefully managed to preserve their value. Losses can easily accrue during the interim period. There is also an emotional price to pay. Survivors can continuously be reminded of the loss of their loved one as the process drags on. A family wealth trust avoids that.

CHAPTER 8

MEDI-CAL VS. MEDICARE

Medi-Cal and Medicare are two entirely different programs. They both stem from federal law but are managed at the state level with federal funding. Anyone who begins looking into long term care options will quickly run into the topics of Medicare and Medi-Cal. Many people confuse the two programs but they're unrelated. Medicare is a federal program that provides basic health insurance for anyone who is 65 and older and those who are under 65 and deemed to be disabled under social security. Medicare is not based on needs or resources. Bill Gates is worth $30 billion but when he turns 65, he will be eligible for Medicare. Participants in Medicare programs are liable for minimum payments, deductibles, and some copayments. Those who are 65 and older can purchase Medicare supplements. Medicare is broken down into what they call parts A, B, C, and D.

Part A is hospital insurance and everyone gets that. Part B is medical insurance and Part C is a Medicare advantage, where you can supplement it with a private insurance plan. Part D is prescription drugs. Medicare does not pay for long term care and that's where the confusion is. After a three-day hospital stay resulting from an injury or an illness, Medicare will pay 100% of skilled nursing for only the first 20 days. For days 21 through 100, it will pay a portion of the cost. After 100 days of skilled nursing, Medicare stops paying altogether. Medicare will pay only for rehabilitative care. Unfortunately, many of our elders are not in long term care for the purposes of rehabilitating. They're there for custodial care because their conditions are chronic. That's when Medicaid or Medi-Cal kicks in. These are joint Federal State Medicaid programs. Medi-Cal and Medicaid are essentially the same program and are designed to pay for the medical costs of low-income people of any age.

Medi-Cal is a need-based program. It's available only to those who meet the state's financial eligibility and medical qualification requirements. Medi-Cal is the main source of financing for most skilled nursing, long term care businesses in California. Medi-Cal will cover most, if not all, of the cost of a skilled nursing facility only if a physician deems that the care is medically necessary. In addition to skill nursing costs, Medi-Cal will also cover essential healthcare services including doctor visits, hospital care, immunizations, some dental care, ambulance services, and drugs. Medicare is federal healthcare insurance and Medi-Cal is not health care insurance. It's a long term care provider, provided that you meet certain resource-based requirements.

In order to qualify for Medi-Cal, a person must be 65 years of age or older or on social security disability. They must have what's called countable assets of $2,000 or less. Meeting the state's financial asset requirement is the most challenging aspect of meeting Medi-Cal eligibility. Medi-Cal will review your income, income taxes, and assets and will assess whether there's a look back or any lifetime gifts.

Does Medi-Cal Cover Nursing Home Care And Assisted Living?

Medi-Cal covers nursing home care and provides for the institutional spouse who has less than $2,000 of countable assets. Medi-Cal, as a general rule, doesn't pay for assisted living, although as of 2009, California has implemented an Assisted Living Waiver Program that has many restrictive requirements. The idea is to keep people out of very expensive long term care facilities. Assisted living, although still expensive, is less costly, so California has introduced the Assisted Living Waiver Program so that if a person meets certain asset requirements, they qualify. Typically, that's a very indigent, no-asset type person. Our typical client would not be eligible.

What Assets Are Exempt From Medi-Cal Eligibility?

We think of Medi-Cal or Medicaid as being only for poor people but the industry has evolved in such a way that this is no longer true. People with a lot of money can matriculate into long term care; you just need to work with an elder law attorney to figure out how to do that. In California, we don't follow the Deficit Reduction Act that was passed in 2005 by George Bush. California hasn't adopted DRA but instead passed SB833. In order to be eligible for Medi-Cal nursing home benefits, one must have $2,000 or less in assets. Medi-Cal does not require that all of its recipients be completely impoverished because certain assets are deemed exempt, meaning that they're not counted for purposes of eligibility.

The main asset that my clients are concerned about is their house. The primary home, in Medicaid and Medi-Cal, is an exempt asset. The DRA has equity limits but those limits don't apply in California. The rule is quite straightforward and generous. If you have a house, it's exempt. It's not considered an asset under any purposes, so long as the house is not probated. In order to protect the house, you have to put it into either a revocable or a irrevocable trust. You have to get it out of the estate. For my clients, I put it into in an Irrevocable Medi-Cal Asset Protection Trust. Sometimes, you have to sell the house and convert it to cash. If you did that in a revocable trust, you just converted an exempt asset to a nonexempt asset and all of that cash becomes a non-exempt asset.

You may wonder why people would sell the home in the first place. Most Bay Area long term care facilities are going to tell you they don't have any Medi-Cal beds. They would much rather rent them out to a long-term care provider at $15,000 than a Medi-Cal reimbursement at $8,500. In order to get into one of the nicer long term care facilities in San Francisco, San Mateo, or Silicon Valley, you're going to have to come in there with about $100,000 to spend down as a private pay. Once you private pay $100,000 and spend them down to $2,000, they're impoverished. Then, by operation of law, they must take Mom as a medical patient and Medi-Cal pays only the $8,500. When you go to these expensive long term care facilities, you'll find many people who are on Medi-Cal but they probably paid $100,000 -$200,000 in private pay to get there. You want to put the house into a Medi-Cal Asset Protection Trust because many times, in order to get Mom or Dad into a facility, you need to convert that house into cash.

There's another very important aspect of Medicaid and Medi-Cal planning called community resource and spouse resource allowance. That's when you're dealing with married couples. Medi-Cal provides special protections for spouses of institutional applicants to make sure that the well spouse will have the minimum support needed to continue living in the community while their other spouse is in long term care. After the Supreme Court ruling in 2015, these benefits are now available to same sex marriages as well. If one spouse is in a long term care facility, the other spouse is entitled to $126,420.

The problem is deciding what to do with the rest of the money. In California, we can stack gifts. It's authorized by the California Welfare and Institution Code. I can stack a lot of money over the course of a month, have the long term care person impoverished, and all the assets go to the surviving spouse.

Other items that you can keep, both in Medicaid and in Medi-Cal, include one automobile, but it has to be of a reasonable value. Also, a second vehicle. You can buy a $100,000 Winnebago with three expanders and that would count. You can also upgrade your house with exempt assets. If you need to put in wheelchair access or remodel the kitchen, those are exempt expenditures. In addition, 401(k) and IRA accounts are exempt, provided that the owner is receiving a distribution. As long as the 401(k) has a designated beneficiary, so it's not probated, that becomes an exempt asset.

CHAPTER 9

WHAT MEDI-CAL OR MEDICARE PLANNING SHOULD I DO TO PROTECT MY ASSETS?

If a spouse is in the process of entering a long term care facility, I suggest that the well spouse immediately consult with an elder law attorney to help assess the situation. The most likely task for an elder law attorney will be to transfer the house into a Medi-Cal Asset Protection Trust, which is an irrevocable trust and will prevent any creditors, including the state of California, from placing any lien on the property for recovery of expenses paid on behalf of the institutional spouse. Some attorneys may advise you to place the house into a revocable trust but if a trustee of the revocable living trust should sell the house and convert the house into cash, it would convert an exempt asset. The house is converted to a nonexempt asset, which can be recovered by the state. Why would anyone want to sell their house in a revocable living trust? Often, it is in order for an institutional spouse to get a bed at a facility. They will often require the family to initially private pay. Then, the institutional spouse, by spending down all assets to $2,000, will automatically roll over to Medi-Cal coverage.

This is a standard industry practice for a number of long term care facilities. It is a big business. They're interested in one thing and that's profit. Medi-Cal can pay for a Medi-Cal patient at the rate of $8,500 per month, where private pay will pay anywhere from $10,000 -$15,000. The long term care facility is more likely to offer a bed to someone who can private pay until they spend down to $2,000. Then, by operation of law, they can't just terminate the person. They shift that room to a Medi-Cal reimbursement rate of $8,500. By law, a tenant cannot be evicted. However, sometimes Medi-Cal patients with dementia or Alzheimer's become violent. That would be the basis to evict either a private-pay or Medi-Cal patient.

What Impact Does The Deficit Reduction Act Or DRA Have On Medi-Cal Planning In California?

The Deficit Reduction Act (DRA) was signed by George Bush in 2005 and maintains several of the pre-DRA benefits. One of the major changes was that Inter-vivos gifts may need lifetime gifting. The stack gifting method that was used to reduce the ineligibility period would run concurrently. Effectively, the big change between the California Medi-Cal SB833 and federal law under DRA is that stack gifting will go away. The current laws we have in California, under Senate Bill 833, will change very soon.

Chapter 10

Do Spouses Automatically Inherit Everything In California?

What a spouse inherits depends on the instrument used to distribute the assets upon the death of the spouse. California is a community property state. If a couple chooses to devise their property by a will and testament, the beneficiaries will receive what is stated in the will because you've got the two community members who have held the asset into a community asset by virtue of preparing that will. However, the decedent doesn't have the legal authority to get half of the community property without the written consent of the other spouse.

If you have a case where the decedent has a will and gifts property to it, the spouse can make a claim to deny the other half of community property going to a beneficiary of the other surviving spouse. For example, you've got a mom and a dad. Dad's got a will and he wants to give all of his house to the local church. He can't do that because, in California, one of the members of the community cannot gift the entire community without the written consent of the other spouse. If this will wasn't signed by the spouse, the spouse has a right to the fair market value. The house might go to the church but the church will have to pay half the value of the property to the spouse.

There is also what's known as the spousal election, allowing the spouse to choose the distribution that effectively benefits the surviving spouse more so than if she were to receive the initial community property distribution. The wife has an election; she can choose to take her half of the house back from the church or they can pay her equal value from other assets in the estate, if such assets are remaining.

Can I Protect My Assets For My Children If My Spouse Remarries After My Death?

A spouse can prepare an AB Trust, a Bypass Trust, and they can prepare a family wealth protection trust or a spendthrift trust. An AB Trust is very effective but clumsy. The property must be split and titled in the name of each of the respective trusts, along with the annual accountings and tax returns that need to be filed for the bypass trust. A simpler way is to set up a family wealth protection trust whereby it is effective as a survivor's trust, so that the administration, upon the death of the deceased settlor, is much easier. However, the protection component that's found in the spendthrift language, which is HEMS (Health, Education, Maintenance, and Support) is an IRS tax provision. If the spendthrift trust has those IRS protections such that the beneficiary receives a distribution only for those standards for the adult children's sub-trust, then the children are protected. Creditors can't touch the assets in the trust.

In order to protect the spouse from remarrying and giving away the family's wealth to another family, the attorney prepares a trust that is also a survivor's trust but with a limited power of appointment. That way, the kids from the first family are protected and they wind up not losing their inheritance. The spendthrift trust is effectively the same thing. A spendthrift trust is not really a trust; it's just asset protection limiting language that you insert into a trust. I would consider inserting Trust Protector language also.

Can We Give Our Assets Away To Our Children?

You can give assets to your children, but it's not a good idea. A Medi-Cal case worker will count the distribution as a disqualifying transfer, which will result in a period of ineligibility. That means the family is going to have to pay about $10,000 per month out of pocket. We can restore that mistake by either obtaining the gift back or drafting a promissory note whereby the person who received the gift agrees to make monthly payments to the donor. Medi-Cal eligibility workers will review the promissory note and the probability that it's a legitimate document to assess its credibility.

I always tell clients that before they gift any property, if they're in the Medi-Cal application process, to first speak with an elder law attorney to ensure that it gets done correctly and that they still meet the eligibility requirements.

How Do I Protect My Assets In A Second Marriage?

A second marriage is one of the trickiest issues in an estate plan. The couple can agree to establish an AB trust whereby at the death of the first spouse, those assets must fund the first trust and those assets are protected from the surviving spouse or anyone else. A bypass trust becomes irrevocable, so no one can get to it. When the survivor dies, the bypass trust goes to the children. The couple could use a survivor's trust with limited power of appointment, which restricts assets of the trust and to whom the survivor can allocate those assets. Usually, the limitation is only to the children of the first trust. I would insert a distribution trustee as well as a trust protector, to make sure that a parent is not unduly influenced by a second spouse.

CHAPTER 11

SHOULD I WORRY ABOUT PROTECTING MY WIFE FROM CREDITORS IN AN ESTATE PLAN?

You should always think about creditors. The typical spendthrift provision limits the authority of the successor trustee from making distributions to a beneficiary with discretion use and the HEMS standard. The Internal Revenue Code 2041 allows such distributions to beneficiaries where there's an outstanding creditor claim and makes those distributions to the beneficiaries without jeopardizing the assets in the trust. If you have a spendthrift trust and there's a HEMS standard, this is discretionary language to the successor trustee that the beneficiary can only get a distribution from the trust so long as the beneficiary is (for example) a 25 year old young adult. If it's for his health, education, maintenance, and welfare, the successor trustee can make a distribution without the creditor seeking to avoid the Bypass Trust all together and attach assets. If the creditor gets knowledge that a distribution has been made to that 25-year-old, they could make a claim against him, individually but not against the Bypass Trust.

We want to make sure that we protect the assets in the trust. As long as the HEMS standards are clearly stated in the trust and the successor trustee does make a distribution, whatever happens to the creditors is up to him. The creditor can't go to court and say that there's a distribution being made. Creditors are prevented from attacking or attaching the assets in the Sub-Trust. Once the creditor becomes knowledgeable that the beneficiary has come into possession, only then can the creditor make a claim. When assets are to be made available to a beneficiary but for the creditor's threat the successor trustee exercises his discretion to withhold assets because of pending creditor claims held by the beneficiary. The distribution is deemed a vested right to the beneficiary, even though the successor trustee hasn't made the distribution. If the language in the Sub-Trust was such that the beneficiary has a vested right, that gives the creditor the right to file, essentially, a demand letter and a creditor notice upon the successor trustee. The successor trustee doesn't want to ignore that because then they may become personally liable.

As a drafting attorney, you don't want to have any language in a Sub-Trust that goes to irresponsible kids bringing in a spendthrift HEMS standard. You don't want to have any language that effectively gives vested rights to certain timing. For example, when child turns 25, distribution occurs and when the child turns 30, distribution occurs. Those become vested rights. The drafting attorney needs to be careful not to do that. You must keep the language very general and not authorize future predestined distributions because that will allow a creditor to make a claim against the trust. These provisions apply to a spouse or a young adult within a family.

Are There Ways To Protect My Spouse When It Comes To My Medi-Cal or Medicaid Assets Affecting Her Eligibility?

If one spouse will soon be entering a long term care facility, that's what we call crisis planning. One would have to create a Medi-Cal Asset Protection Trust (MAPT) immediately, transfer the house into it, move all assets that are nonexempt assets, and stack gift them to family members. Or, just spend them down. Get the house into a MAPT trust immediately and stack gifts or convert nonexempt assets into exempt assets, such as improving the house. This plan only works if there is a written, completed estate plan.

Many married couples have no estate plan at all. If there is no plan, the attorney must rush into court and file a 3100 petition to get a substituted judgment to move the assets out of the name of the institutional spouse and into the name of the well spouse. That 3100 petition is probably going to cost them $5,000, when they could have created an estate plan for $2,500.

CHAPTER 12

PROBLEMS THAT MAY ARISE WHEN DOING PROPER ESTATE PLANNING FOR BENEFICIARIES

A beneficiary may have a creditor problem or have special needs, or there's just not proper planning. If a couple doesn't have an estate plan at all or they have an estate plan with ineffective gifting language, their lawyer has to go into probate court and file a 3100 petition, which is very expensive. Only getting an Order under a substituted judgment would authorize the attorney to save the assets. Most estate planning attorneys don't know anything about this, as they don't practice in the area of elder law. You need to go to an elder law attorney who is also an estate planning attorney.

What Should We Consider When Looking At How To Structure The Inheritance Of Our Children And Grandchildren?

You can set up a Sub-Trust and that trust will manage the fund until your child reaches age 25. It is known that the prefrontal cortex develops slower in males than in females. At about age 25, that prefrontal cortex, which is the executive function portion of the brain, is finally fully formed in most men. That is why 25 is a common age at which to make a distribution. I would never suggest a distribution at age 18.

If you have children who are 25 and still don't have maturity, we can build into the Sub-Trust spendthrift language with the HEMS standard. And, we can put some restrictive discretionary language that the successor trustee will not be the child. It could be another child. I often insert what's called a Trust Protector, which is a disinterested person who is not a party to the family. The correct language requires contacting an individual lawyer, a CPA, or going to a trust department.

A professional fiduciary would act as a Trustor Protector. When it comes to marriages, I would put in some spendthrift language and have a Trustor Protector who's a disinterested party. In marriages, what we're trying to protect is the surviving spouse, which is usually the wife. I'll put in some spendthrift, some HEMS, and I'll have a Trustor Protector to protect her and her children from a future second spouse. I'll also limit the power of appointment from a general to a limited, so that there's no misbehaving from future spouses. The same setup can be used for heirs who have drug or alcohol addictions, even to the extent of requiring drug testing before a distribution can be made.

How Can We Ensure That Our Disabled Child Will Be Taken Care Of When We Die?

In all trusts in which I have a child with special needs, I'll insert a special needs trust for that child, which will be a long term ongoing trust and will require annual tax returns and accountings. There's a particular language in special needs trusts because we want to make sure that special needs trust children will have access to Medi-Cal and, potentially, Medicare. We don't want to lose the possibility of free medical care or SSI for that person by allowing them to inherit too much money. A special needs trust carries legal significance. What you're trying to do in the special needs trust is not to disqualify the beneficiary from receiving governmental benefits.

If we want to make sure that government benefits are maintained, the money will go into special needs trust and there will be a separate, nonfamily member successor trustee who will oversee and make sure that it is done correctly. The special needs child will be able to receive distributions for certain housing and for transportation. As long as the distribution standard meets California rules, the state can't come after any of the assets. This is called a third party special needs trust.

There's also a first party special needs trust. When you have a disabled person who's on Medi-Cal and SSI who, all of a sudden, receives an inheritance check, it can immediately disqualify him. If he has good advice, he will set up a first party self-settled special needs trust with an elder law attorney. The only difference is that he can draw on it, pay for services needed, and get government benefits. When he dies, anything left over goes to the state for services provided.

CHAPTER 13

CAN I DIRECTLY LEAVE MY IRA TO MY GRANDCHILDREN?

The general rule is that you can leave a spouse your IRA or 401(k). The surviving spouse can stretch to that amount over the course of that person's own life. If I am 80 and my wife is 50 and I die and leave her my 401(k), she can pick up that 401(k) at age 50. She doesn't have to take the RMDs (Required Minimum Distributions) that I have been taking as an 80 year old. She can stretch out the accrual of that IRA until she reaches age 70.5, provided Congress doesn't change that. A Stretch IRA is an estate planning strategy which extends the tax diversion status from an inherited IRA when it passes to a spouse or kids. It allows continued tax deferred growth in the IRA.

An IRA can be passed down from generation to generation while the beneficiaries enjoy tax deferred and tax free growth. The term stretch does also represent a specific type of IRA, rather than a financial strategy that allows people to stretch out the life of the inherited IRA. Stretching out an IRA can give funds in the IRA more time to compound, tax deferred. This provides the opportunity to grow the funds significantly for future generations. With a traditional IRA, the owner has asked to begin taking the required minimum distributions by April 1st of the year after turning 70 and a half. Those RMDs are calculated by the IRS and the account must be taken no later than December 31st of the previous year.

Dividing by the number of years left in the owner's life expectancy, you can reference the IRS uniform lifetime table. Each year, the RMD is calculated by dividing the account balance by their remaining life expectancy. Non-spouse heirs of any age, regardless of the type of the IRA, must take the RMDs based on their life expectancies. The rules for inherited

IRAs are different for spouses and non-spouses. The younger the beneficiary, the lower the RMD, which allows more funds to remain in the IRA to stretch over a lifetime. This is why stretch IRAs are passed to younger members of the family.

Wealthier retirees, who know that their spouse will have enough money for retirement, will use stretch IRAs to maintain their family's wealth by naming the youngest person in their family as a beneficiary. The remaining sum of the IRA will continue to grow, tax deferred. However, not all IRAs allow stretch strategy. Clients should check with their financial advisors to determine if their beneficiaries can be allowed to take big distributions over their life expectancy. Stretch IRA is especially beneficial when used for Roth IRAs because distributions are usually tax free.

Establishing An IRA Inheritance Trust

The industry of estate planning has come up with all of these new terms of art, like asset protection trust and wealth family trusts. They're really all the same thing. An IRA Inheritance Trust is a little different. The primary reason is to assert control over post death distribution, plus limit access to the inheritance. You're not saving taxes by naming a trust like this. In fact, it's quite possible to pay more in taxes, even though the trust is properly designed. An IRA Inheritance Trust is a non-tax savings device used to provide the trustee owner with the authority to control distributions, often for misbehaving children.

Certainly, in naming a trust that fits a child's overall objective, an advisor should advise, with the co-counsel of an elder law attorney, that the trust qualifies as a look back or see through trust. The IRS will look through the trust and treat the trust beneficiaries as the IRA's direct beneficiary. Although the trust remains the direct owner of the IRA, this allows the heirs to take advantage of favorable minimum distribution rules that apply to individuals designated as beneficiaries. For beneficiaries who have a life expectancy, never move an IRA asset into a trust. Doing so will only result in a taxable event on the entire IRA balance. Instead, name the trust as a beneficiary of the IRA.

If you have a non-beneficiary receive a distribution, they can pick it up at their rate. If an IRA or a trust inherits an IRA, there's a five-year distribution rule, so the beneficiaries are going to have to pick up all of them. They are going to have to pick up 20% per year and that's not the best way to go. If you put it into the IRA, there's a little spendthrift protection. Also, if it qualifies as an IRA Trust, the IRS perceives it as a see-through entity and the individual beneficiaries have the same benefits. The law reads that if there are multiple beneficiaries, you have to pick it up and stretch it out at the age of the eldest beneficiary.

What Role Can A Trustee Play In Handling The Inheritance For Our Children?

The main role of a trustee of an IRA Inheritance Trust, is to assess the maturity and the business acumen of the beneficiary; to assess whether that person is mature enough to receive a distribution. If the Trustee is of the opinion that the young individual is not yet ready to receive a distribution, the Trustee has the authority to withhold.

Are There Preventive Measures We Can Take To Protect Our Children's Inheritance From Divorce, Second Marriages/Step Children, Etc.?

Prenuptial actions are a very responsible action to take. It identifies whose property is for whom and what is separate property and what is community property. From a side of things, an AB trust may be best suited.

Should I Sell Them My Home? Should I Gift It Directly To The Beneficiaries Before My Death?

If we're dealing with Medi-Cal protection, selling the home is malpractice because you're converting an "exempt asset" not subject to recovery to a "non-exempt asset" which is subject to recovery.

When Moving And Protecting My Assets In Life, What Taxes Do I Need To Be Aware Of?

There's no tax when moving into a trust. Don't change title. Try your best not to gift inter vivos transfer meaning while living because the donee will receive reduced tax-basis and large cap-gain exposure.

How Can We Minimize Those Taxes?

As a general rule, highly appreciated property should not be gifted during life so as to obtain "step-up" basis.

Also, you do not need to be concerned with taxes your beneficiaries may incur after your death.

How Often Should We Revisit and Revise Our Estate Planning During Life?

I advise my clients to call me once there's a death in the family, perhaps a divorce, or if a child is diagnosed with a drug use disorder, that is a good time to revisit your estate plan. I can quickly amend the Trust to protect both the adult child and the family as circumstances change. There are things we can do to protect the family when this happens, but the client needs to inform me. Laws change frequently which is why I email my client base every month with my newsletter that alerts them to changes regarding Medi-Cal, Social Security, and federal & state income taxes. I encourage my clients to call me anytime during the day to discuss these issues at no cost. I NEVER charge a client for a telephone call.

What Conversation Do You Encourage Your Clients To Have With Their Beneficiaries, If Any, Regarding Assets And Inheritance They May Receive?

I highly encourage my clients to discuss their estate plan with their beneficiaries; namely their adult children. I prefer this approach as it alerts both the parents and children of any potential dispute they may have and to address those issues while everyone is still alive to talk about it. It's better to get those issues on the table now rather than wait 10 or 20 years only to litigate these disputes that could have been more appropriately addressed while mom and dad where alive. I just like the idea of having no surprises at death. It's better for everyone.

What Are The Top 6 Estate Planning Mistakes?

If you're like most people, you have the best of intentions with regard to how you want your estate distributed when you die, or your affairs handled should you become incapacitated. Unfortunately, without proper planning, your best intentions may not be enough. Here are six of the most common estate planning mistakes people make:

1. **Doing it yourself. Bad Idea.** It is tempting to try to save money by using a do-it-yourself online service or just writing something up yourself, but these poorly drafted documents may only cost you or your heirs' additional money in the end. It is impossible to know, without a legal education and years of experience, what the right legal solution is to any particular situation and what planning

opportunities are available. If there is anything about a family situation that's not commonplace, using a DIY estate planning program means taking a *LARGE RISK* that can affect one's family for generations to come. And only an attorney can determine whether a particular situation qualifies as commonplace. The problems created by not getting competent legal advice probably won't be borne by the person creating the will, but they may well be shouldered by the person's children and grandchildren.

2. **Failing to plan**. The biggest mistake is failing to create a plan in the first place. Without an estate plan, your assets will be distributed according to the law in the state where you live. Usually, if you are married, your spouse is entitled to a portion of your estate and the rest is divided among other relatives. If you are single, your estate may go to your children, parents, or siblings. If you have absolutely no living relatives, then your estate will go to the state. This is probably not what you want to happen to your assets. In addition, without an estate plan, you have no way to name who will be the guardian of your children or who will act for you if you become incapacitated

3. **Not planning for disability**. A properly drafted estate plan not only specifies what will happen to your assets when you die; it also plans for what happens if you become incapacitated. It is important to have documents, such as a power of attorney and health care proxy that appoint someone to act on your behalf if you can't act for yourself. Elder law attorneys know what Medi-Cal legal language is necessary to gift assets so that Medi-Cal doesn't recover against the estate upon death of the Medi-Cal applicant. LegalZoom has no clue about this.

4. **Failing to fund a trust**. Once you draft an estate plan, you aren't done. If your estate plan includes a trust, you need to actually fund the trust, by retitling assets in the name of the trust, or the trust will be useless.

5. **Not checking your beneficiary designations**. You should periodically review your retirement plan beneficiary designations to make sure they aren't outdated. Retirement accounts do not follow your will or trust—they are distributed according to the forms you fill out with the insurance company. You need to make sure you have named a beneficiary and the beneficiary is who you want it to be.

6. **Not reviewing the plan.** Once you've got an estate plan in place, it is important to keep it up to date. Circumstances change over time and your estate plan needs to keep up with these changes. Major changes that may affect your plan include getting married or divorced, having children, or experiencing an increase or decrease in assets. Even if you don't have any major changes, you should review your plan periodically to make sure it still expresses your wishes.

Four Steps to Take Immediately After an Alzheimer's Diagnosis

If you or a loved one has been diagnosed with Alzheimer's disease or other form of dementia, it is important to start planning immediately. There are several essential legal documents to help you once you become incapacitated, but if you don't already have them in place, you need to act quickly after a diagnosis.

Having dementia does not mean an individual is not mentally competent to make planning decisions. The person signing documents must have "testamentary capacity," which means he or she must understand the implications of what is being signed. Simply having a form of mental illness or disease does not mean that you automatically lack the required mental capacity. All forms of dementia are progressive; however, a person who has periods of lucidity, may still be competent to sign planning documents.

The following are some essential documents for someone diagnosed with dementia:

- **Power of Attorney.** A power of attorney is the most important estate planning document for someone who has been diagnosed with Alzheimer's disease or some other form of dementia. A power of attorney allows you to appoint someone to make decisions on your behalf once you become incapacitated. Without a power of attorney, your family would be unable to pay your bills or manage your household without going to court and getting a conservatorship, which can be a time-consuming and expensive process. Furthermore, have an Elder Law attorney draft Medi-Cal planning and gifting language that authorizes your agent to legally shift assets to qualify for Long-Term care without impoverishing a surviving spouse.

- **Health Care Proxy.** A health care proxy, like a power of attorney, allows you to appoint someone else to act as your agent for medical decisions. It will ensure that your medical treatment instructions are carried out. In general, a health care proxy takes effect only when you require medical treatment and a physician determines that you are unable to communicate your wishes concerning treatment.
- **Medical Directive or Living Will**. Medical directives and living wills explain what type of care you would like if you are unable to direct your own care. A medical directive can include a health care proxy, or it can be a separate document. It may contain directions to refuse or remove life support in the event you are in a coma or a vegetative state or it may provide instructions to use all efforts to keep you alive, no matter what the circumstances.
- **Will and Other Estate Planning Documents**. In addition to making sure you have people to act for you and your wishes are clear, you should make sure your estate plan is up to date, or if you don't have an estate plan, you

should draw one up. Your estate plan directs who will receive your property when you die. Once you are deemed incapacitated, you will no longer be able to create an estate plan. An estate plan usually consists of a will, and often a trust as well. Your will is your legally binding statement on who will receive your property when you die, while a trust is a mechanism for passing on your property outside of probate. In addition to executing these documents, it is also important to create a plan for long-term care. Long-term care is expensive and draining for family members. Be sure to have a Trust if you believe that a family member with dementia may be entering long-term care. Developing a plan now for what type of care you would like and how to pay for it will help your family later on.

CHAPTER 14

CONCLUSION

Thank for taking the time to read this book. It says volumes about your desire to manage your estate upon your death and that you value quality information. This book was not intended to be a legal treatise but rather an executive summary of a voluminous subject matter that was presented in a way that most readers can quickly grasp concepts and appreciate the quick read. If you are a resident of California. I invite you to call our office and schedule an appointment to sit down with us so that we can review your current estate plan and provide some feedback as to what adjustments might be in YOUR best interests. We offer a free 30-minute telephone or office visit to discuss these issues.

What Is The Next Step?

Make an appointment with the Law Office of Jeffrey Hall, PC, to discuss what the next steps are to design a plan that is unique and appropriate for your family circumstances. Call 925-230-9002, or email at info@HallLawGropup.com, or visit him at his website at www.HallLawGroup.com. Mr. Hall offers a free 30-minute telephone consultation.

INDEX

NOTES

Made in the USA
Monee, IL
05 November 2026

67385068R00057